M000092386

Aunt Phil's Trunk Volume Four

Student Workbook

Bringing Alaska's history alive!

By
Laurel Downing Bill

Special credit and much appreciation to Nicole Cruz for her diligent efforts to create the best student workbook and teacher guide available for Alaska history studies.

Aunt Phil's Trunk LLC, Anchorage, Alaska
www.auntphilstrunk.com

International Standard Book Number 978-1-940479-35-4
Printed and bound in the United States of America.

First Printing 2017
First Printing Second Edition 2017
First Printing Third Edition 2018

Photo credits on the front cover, from top left: Native shaman with totem, Alaska State Library, Case and Draper Collection, ASL-P-39-782; Eskimo boy, Alaska State Library, Skinner Foundation, ASL-P44-11-002; Prospector, Alaska State Library, Skinner Foundation, ASL-P44-03-15; Athabascan woman, Anchorage Museum of History and Art, Crary–Henderson Collection, AMHA-b62-1-571; Gold miners, Alaska State Library, Harry T.Becker Collection, ASL-P67-052; Chilkoot Pass, Alaska State Library, Eric A. Hegg Collection, ASL-P124-04; Seal hunter, Alaska State Library, George A. Parks Collection, ASL-P240-210; Women mending boat, Alaska State Library, Rev. Samuel Spriggs Collection, ASL-P320-60; Students in class, Alaska State Library, Wickersham State Historical Site, ASL-P277-015-029.

TABLE OF CONTENTS

TABLE OF CONTENTS

Welcome to *Aunt Phil's Trunk Volume Four* Workbook for Students!

Read the chapters associated with each Unit. Then complete the lessons for that Unit to get a better understanding of Alaska's people and the events that helped shape Alaska's future.

I hope you enjoy your journey into Alaska's past from the years 1935 to 1960.

Laurel Downing Bill, author

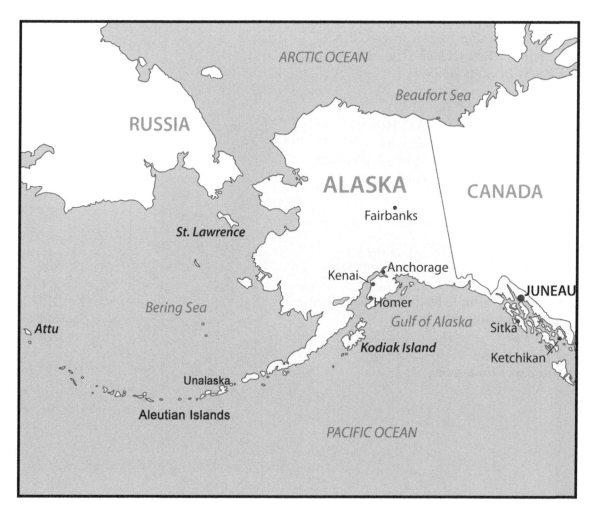

Instructions for using the Aunt Phil's Trunk Alaska History Curriculum

The *Aunt Phil's Trunk* Alaska History Curriculum is designed to be used in grades 4-8. High school students can use this curriculum, also, by taking advantage of the essay and enrichment activities throughout the book. The next few pages give further instruction on how to use this curriculum with middle school students, high school students and in classroom settings.

This curriculum can be taught in multiple grade levels by having your older students complete all reading, study guide work and enrichment activities independently. Students of all grade levels can participate in daily oral review by playing games like Jeopardy or Around the World.

This curriculum was developed so that students not only learn about Alaska's past, but they will have fun in the process. After every few lessons, they can test their knowledge through word scramble, word search and crossword puzzles.

Notes for parents with younger students:

Enrichment Activities occasionally direct your child to watch educational videos on YouTube.com or link to other Websites to learn more about the topic that they are reading about in the lesson. You may want to supervise younger children while they are using the Internet to be sure that they do not click on any inappropriate content. This also provides a good opportunity to discuss Internet safety with your child/children.

How to use this workbook at home

Aunt Phil's Trunk Alaska History Curriculum is designed to be used in grades 4-8. High school students can use this curriculum, also, by taking advantage of the essay and enrichment activities throughout the book. The next page gives further instruction on how to use this curriculum with high school students.

This curriculum can be taught in multiple grade levels by having your older students complete all reading, study guide work and enrichment activities independently. Students of all grade levels can participate in daily oral review by playing games like Jeopardy or Around the World.

For Middle School Students:

1. **Facts to Know:** Read this section in the study guide with your student(s) before reading the chapter to get familiar with new terms that they will encounter in the reading.

2. **Read the chapter:** Read one chapter aloud to your student(s) or have them read it aloud to you. Older students may want to read independently.

3. **Comprehension Questions:** Younger students may answer the comprehension questions orally or write down their answers in the study guide. Use these questions to test your student(s) comprehension of the chapter. Older students should answer all questions in written form.

4. **Discussion Questions:** Have your student(s) answer these questions in a few sentences orally. Come up with follow-up questions to test your student(s) understanding of the material. Older students may answer discussion questions in written essay form.

5. **Map Work:** Some chapters will contain a map activity for your student(s) to learn more about the geography of the region that they are learning about.

6. **Enrichment and Online References:** (Optional) Assign enrichment activities as you see fit. Many of the online references are from the Alaska Humanities Forum website (http://www.akhistorycourse.org). We highly recommend this website for additional information, project ideas, etc.

7. **Unit Review:** At the end of a unit, your student will complete Unit Review questions and word puzzles in the study guide. Students should review all the chapters in the unit before completing the review. Parents may want to assist younger students with the word puzzles.

8. **Unit Test:** (Optional) There is an optional test that you can administer to your student(s) after they have completed all the unit work.

How to use this workbook for high school

1. **Facts to Know:** Your student(s) should read this section in the study guide before reading the chapter to get familiar with new terms that they will encounter.

2. **Read the chapter:** Your student(s) can read aloud or independently.

3. **Comprehension Questions:** Use these questions to test your student(s) comprehension of the chapter. Have your high schoolers write out their answers in complete sentences.

4. **Discussion Questions:** Have your student(s) answer these questions in a few sentences orally or write out their answer in essay form.

5. **Map Work:** Some chapters will contain a map activity for your student(s) to learn more about the geography of the region that they are learning about.

6. **Enrichment and Online References:** Once your high schooler has completed all the reading and study guide material for the chapter, assign additional reading from the enrichment material using the online links or book lists. Encourage your student(s) to explore topics of interest to them.

Many of the online references are from the Alaska Humanities Forum website. We highly recommend this website for additional information, project ideas, etc.

7. **Unit Review:** At the end of a unit, your student will complete Unit Review questions and word puzzles in their study guide. Students should review all the chapters in the unit before completing the review.

8. **Unit Test:** (Optional) There is an optional test that you can administer to your student(s) after they have completed all the unit work.

9. **Oral Presentation:** (Optional) Assign a 5-minute oral presentation on any topic in the reading. Encourage your student(s) to utilize the additional books and online resources to supplement the information in the textbook. Set aside a classroom day for your student(s) to share their presentations.

10. **Historical Inquiry Project:** Your student(s) will choose a topic from the reading to learn more about and explore that topic through library visits, museum trips, visiting historical sites, etc.

Visit https://www.nhd.org/how-enter-contest for detailed information on how to put together a historical inquiry project. You may even want to have your students enter the national contest.

How to use this workbook in the classroom

Aunt Phil's Trunk Alaska History Curriculum was created for homeschooling families, but it also can work well in a co-op or classroom setting. Here are some suggestions on how to use this curriculum in a classroom setting. Use what works best for your classroom.

1. **Facts to Know:** The teacher introduces students to the Facts to Know to familiarize the students with terms that they will encounter in the chapter.

2. **Read the chapter:** The teacher can read the chapter aloud while the students follow along in the book. Students also may take turns reading aloud.

3. **Comprehension Questions:** The teacher uses these questions to test the students' comprehension of the chapter. Students should write out the answers in their study guide and the teacher can review the answers with the students in class.

4. **Discussion Questions:** The teacher chooses a few students to answer these questions orally during class. Alternatively, teachers can assign these questions to be completed in essay form individually and answers can be shared during class.

5. **Map Work:** Some chapters will contain a map activity for your students to learn more about the geography of the region that they are learning about. Have your students complete the activity independently.

6. **Enrichment and Online References:** Assign enrichment activities as you see fit.

7. **Daily Review:** Students should review the material for the current unit daily. You can do this by asking review questions orally. Playing review games like Jeopardy or Around the World is a fun way to get your students excited about the material.

8. **Unit Review:** At the end of a unit, your student will complete Unit Review questions and word puzzles in the study guide. Have students review all the unit chapters before completing.

9. **Unit Test:** (Optional) There is an optional test that you can administer to your students after they have completed all the unit work.

10. **Oral Presentation:** (Optional) Assign a 5-minute oral presentation on any topic in the reading. Encourage your students to utilize the additional books and online resources to supplement the information in the textbook. Set aside a classroom day for students to share their presentations.

11. **Historical Inquiry Project:** Your student(s) will choose a topic from the reading to learn more about and explore that topic through library visits, museum trips, visiting historical sites, etc.

Visit https://www.nhd.org/how-enter-contest for detailed information on how to put together a historical inquiry project. You may even want to have your students enter the national contest.

How to grade the assignments

Our rubric grids are designed to make it easy for you to grade your students' essays, oral presentations and enrichment activities. Encourage your students to look at the rubric grid before completing an assignment as a reminder of what an exemplary assignment should include.

You can mark grades for review questions, essay tests and extra credit assignments on the last page of each unit in the student workbook. Use these pages as a tool to help your students track their progress and improve their assignment grades.

Unit Review Questions

Students are given one point for each correct review and fill-in-the-blank question. Mark these points on the last page of each unit in the student workbook.

Essay Test Questions

Students will complete two or more essay questions at the end of each unit. These questions are designed to test your students' knowledge about the key topics of each unit. You can give a student up to 20 points for each essay.

Students are graded on a scale of 1-5 in four categories:

1) Understanding the topic
2) Answering all questions completely and accurately
3) Neatness and organization
4) Grammar, spelling and punctuation

Use the essay rubric grid on page 11 as a guide to give up to 5 points in each category for every essay. Mark these points for each essay on the last page of each Unit Review in the student workbook.

Word Puzzles

Word puzzles that appear at the end of the Unit Reviews count for 5 points, or you can give partial points if the student does not fill in the puzzle completely. Mark these points under the extra category on the last page of each Unit Review in the student workbook.

Enrichment Activities

Most lessons contain an enrichment activity for further research and interaction with the information in the lesson. You can make these optional or assign every activity as part of the lesson. You can use the provided rubric on page 12 to give up to 5 points for each assignment. Mark these points under the extra category on the last page of each Unit Review in the student workbook.

Oral Presentations

You have the option of assigning oral presentations on any topic from the unit as extra credit. If you choose to assign oral presentations, you can use the provided rubric to grade your student on content and presentation skills. Discuss what presentation skills you will be grading your student on before each presentation day.

Some examples of presentation skills you can grade on include:

– Eye contact with the audience
– Proper speaking volume
– Using correct posture
– Speaking clearly

Use the oral presentation rubric grid on page 12 as a guide to give up to 10 points. Mark these points under the extra category on the last page of each Unit Review in the student workbook.

Rubric for Essay Questions

	Beginning 1	Needs Improvement 2	Acceptable 3	Accomplished 4	Exemplary 5
Demonstrates Understanding of the topic	Student's work shows incomplete understanding of the topic	Student's work shows slight understanding of the topic	Student's work shows a basic understanding of the topic	Student's work shows complete understanding of the topic	Student's work demonstrates strong insight about the topic
Answered questions completely and accurately	Student's work did not address all of the questions	Student answered all of the questions with some accuracy	Student answered all questions with close to 100% accuracy	Student answered all questions with 100% accuracy	Student goes beyond the questions to demonstrate knowledge of the topic
Essay is neat and well organized	Student's work is sloppy and unorganized	Student's work is somewhat neat and organized	Student's essay is neat and somewhat organized	Student's work is well organized and neat	Student demonstrates extra care in organizing the essay and making it neat
Essay contains good grammar and spelling	Student's work is poorly written and hard to understand	Student's work contains some grammar, spelling and punctuation mistakes, but not enough to impede understanding	Student's work contains only 1 or 2 grammar, spelling or punctuation errors	Student's work contains no grammar, spelling or punctuation errors	Student's work is extremely well-written

Rubric for Oral Presentations

	Beginning 1	Needs Improvement 2	Acceptable 3	Accomplished 4	Exemplary 5
Preparation	Student did not prepare for the presentation	Student was somewhat prepared for the presentation	Student was prepared for the presentation and addressed the topic	Student was well-prepared for the presentation and addressed important points about the topic	Student prepared an excellent presentation that exhibited creativity and originality
Presentation Skills	Student demonstrated poor presentation skills (no eye contact, low volume, appears disinterested in the topic)	Student made some effort to demonstrate presentation skills (eye contact, spoke clearly, engaged audience, etc.)	Student demonstrated acceptable presentation skills (eye contact, spoke clearly, engaged audience, etc.)	Student demonstrated good presentation skills (eye contact, spoke clearly, engaged audience, etc.)	Student demonstrated strong presentation skills (eye contact, spoke clearly, engaged audience, etc.)

Rubric for Enrichment Activities

	Beginning 1	Needs Improvement 2	Acceptable 3	Accomplished 4	Exemplary 5
	Student's work is incomplete or inaccurate	Student's work is complete and somewhat inaccurate	Student completed the assignment with accuracy	Student's work is accurate, complete, neat and well-organized	Student demonstrates exceptional creativity or originality

UNIT 1: WORLD WAR II ERUPTS

LESSON 1: DEFENSE FOR ALASKA

FACTS TO KNOW

Pearl Harbor – Hawaiian port that was attacked with bombs by Japan on December 7, 1941

President Franklin D. Roosevelt – The 32nd president of the United States who declared war on Japan after the bombing of Pearl Harbor

COMPREHENSION QUESTIONS

1) How many Americans were killed during the attack on Pearl Harbor? What other damage was done? _____

_____

_____

_____

2) Why were tensions high between the United States and Japan by 1940?

_____

_____

_____

_____

3) What kind of military presence was in Alaska before the bombing of Pearl Harbor?

_____

_____

_____

_____

4) Explain the Lend-Lease Act. _____

_____

_____

_____

5) How did the United States benefit from the Lend-Lease Act after Japan attacked Pearl Harbor? _____

_____
_____
_____

DISCUSSION QUESTION

(Discuss this question with your teacher or write your answer in essay form below. Use additional paper if necessary.)

Why did the Army close all of its forts in Alaska between 1921-1925?

_____
_____
_____
_____
_____
_____
_____
_____
_____
_____
_____
_____
_____
_____
_____
_____

ENRICHMENT ACTIVITY

Read eyewitness accounts from Pearl Harbor by visiting the link below. Next, it is your turn to interview an older relative or community member about their memories of Pearl Harbor. Write down at least three questions to ask during your interview. http://teacher.scholastic.com/pearl/eyewits.htm

LEARN MORE

Learn more about the attack on Pearl Harbor by visiting https://www.history.navy.mil/browse-by-topic/wars-conflicts-and-operations/world-war-ii/1941/pearl-harbor.html

UNIT 1: WORLD WAR II ERUPTS

LESSON 2: RUSSIA'S SECRET MISSION

FACTS TO KNOW

Ladd Field – Alaska's first airfield, named after Maj. Arthur Ladd who was killed in a plane crash in South Carolina in 1935

Soviet – A citizen and/or soldier of the former Union of Soviet Socialist Republics

Henry H. Arnold – Commander of U.S. Army Air Forces who recommended that an air base be built at Fairbanks

COMPREHENSION QUESTIONS

1) Why was a stronger military presence in Alaska important to America's defense?

_____

_____

_____

_____

2) What part did Henry Arnold play in increasing military presence in Alaska?

_____

_____

_____

_____

3) What was the cold weather experimental station? _____

_____

_____

_____

_____

4) What secret mission made Ladd Field a vital link between America and the Soviet Union? _____

_____

_____

_____

_____

5) What was life like for Russian soldiers at Ladd Field?

_____

_____

_____

_____

DISCUSSION QUESTION

(Discuss this question with your teacher or write your answer in essay form below. Use additional paper if necessary.)

Why did Russia want to keep the Lend-Lease Agreement with the United States a secret?

_____

_____

_____

_____

_____

_____

_____

_____

_____

_____

_____

_____

_____

_____

_____

ENRICHMENT ACTIVITY

Take some time to show your appreciation to those who risk their lives to protect our country.

Note to teacher: Visit the link below. Choose one project to do as a class or invite students to choose individual projects from the list.

https://service-project-ideas.jimdo.com/service-project-ideas/military-veterans/

LEARN MORE

Read more about the long history of Ladd Field by visiting https://www.army.mil/article/41754/ladd-field-has-long-history/

UNIT 1: WORLD WAR II ERUPTS

LESSON 3: ARMY BASE REVITALIZES ANCHORAGE

FACTS TO KNOW

Fort Richardson – The first Army base in Anchorage built in 1940; later named Elmendorf Air Force Base (recently renamed again to Joint Base Elmendorf-Richardson – called J-BER)

Col. Simon Bolivar Buckner – Led the Alaska Defense Force in Anchorage

COMPREHENSION QUESTIONS

1) What was Anchorage like before the military began building Fort Richardson in 1940?

_____

_____

_____

_____

2) What issues did Anchorage face with the large stream of workers coming in to work on the army base? _____

_____

_____

_____

3) What monumental task did Col. Simon Buckner face? _____

_____

_____

_____

4) Why was construction of Fort Richardson slow? _____

_____

_____

_____

5) How did life change for Alaskan's after the attack on Pearl Harbor in 1941?

_____

_____

_____

_____

DISCUSSION QUESTION

(Discuss this question with your teacher or write your answer in essay form below. Use additional paper if necessary.)

How did Fort Richardson "revitalize" Anchorage?

_____

_____

_____

_____

_____

_____

_____

_____

_____

_____

_____

_____

_____

_____

_____

LEARN MORE

Read more about the military history of Alaska by visiting:
http://www.akhistorycourse.org/alaskas-cultures/military-in-alaska

TIME TO REVIEW

Review Chapters 1-3 of your book before moving on the Unit Review. See how many questions you can answer without looking at your book.

UNIT 1: WORLD WAR II ERUPTS

REVIEW LESSONS 1-3

Write down what you remember about:

Pearl Harbor _____

_____

President Franklin D. Roosevelt _____

_____

Ladd Field _____

_____

Soviet _____

_____

Henry H. Arnold _____

_____

Fort Richardson _____

_____

Col. Simon Bolivar Buckner _____

_____

Fill in the blanks:

1) On December _____, one day after the early morning attack on
_____, U.S. President _____ went before both houses of
Congress to request a declaration of war against _____.

2) "If we would provide an adequate _____ for the United States, we must
have _____ to dominate the North Pacific," said U.S. Secretary of State
_____ in a speech to convince Congress of the value of buying
_____ in the mid-1860s.

3) Prior to the opening of _____ in 1940, Alaska was a vast, undefended territory. The only active military installation was the _____, located in Haines. There were no military _____.

4) In the fall of 1942, the United States and the _____ signed a _____ agreement that made _____ a vital link in a secret mission to get American-made _____ to the _____ front. _____ Field became the official _____ transfer point between the two nations.

5) The Americans wanted to fly the planes on to Siberia, but _____ leader _____ said no. He didn't want any appearance of _____ collaboration in the Far East, as his country and _____ were not at war and he wanted to avoid any incidents that might incite the _____.

6) Before the military began building the original _____ in 1940, which later became _____ Force Base, _____ was a typical small town. In 1938, the city's 4,000 residents had no _____ roads, no street or _____ lights and the police chief _____ by using his stopwatch.

7) Congress finally realized that _____, at the time an ally of Germany, only lay _____ miles away from Alaska at the point where the _____ Peninsula and the _____ Peninsula reach out toward each other.

8) Following the attack on _____ by _____ on Dec. 7, 1941, progress on the base's construction ramped up and life changed dramatically for Alaskans. Residents had to tape _____ at night or _____ their windows black. _____ were turned off, and cars drove through the winter darkness with only parking lights to illuminate the way. When _____ sounded, residents were to leave their homes and hide in the _____.

Alaska & World War II
Word Scramble Puzzle
Unscramble the words below

1. prlae rboarh

    U.S. President Franklin D. Roosevelt declared war on Japan after it bombed this location

2. khlooitc

    Only military barracks in Alaska when United States entered World War II

3. iaskt

    In 1937, the U.S. Navy established a small seaplane base at this Southeast town

4. hcdnsirora

    The U.S. Army began building this military base near Anchorage in 1940

5. addl

    This cold-weather experimental station in Fairbanks welcomed its first U.S. Army Air Corps troops in 1940

6. isrnusa

    American military turned airplanes over to these pilots in Fairbanks in lend-lease program

7. cceletri uwaeerrdn

    Development of these at cold-weather experimental station was a hit with aviators

8. cknrbeu

    This military officer took command of the Alaska Defense Force

9. feneodlrm

    Name of military airfield created near Anchorage

10. **evere**

    Alaska bush pilot who flew more than 1,100 tons of equipment and 300 men from Anchorage to military sites in 1941

UNIT 1: WORLD WAR II ERUPTS

UNIT TEST

Choose *two* of the following questions to answer in paragraph form. Use as much detail as possible to completely answer the question. Use extra paper in back of the book if needed.

1) What major event in U.S. history caused the government to push for stronger military presence in Alaska? How did this event change everyday life for Alaskans?

2) Describe the secret mission between America and Russia. Why was this mission kept secret?

3) Why was Alaska an ideal location for a U.S. Army base? In what city did the military build an Army base in 1940? How did the Army base revitalize this city?

_____

_____

_____

_____

_____

_____

_____

_____

_____

_____

_____

_____

_____

_____

_____

_____

_____

_____

_____

_____

_____

Aunt Phil's Trunk Volume Four

UNIT 1: WORLD WAR II ERUPTS

Review Questions   _____ (possible   7 pts.)
Fill-the-Blanks   _____ (possible   8 pts.)

Unit Test

Essay 1
Demonstrates understanding of the topic   _____ (possible 5 pts.)
Answered the questions completely and accurately   _____ (possible 5 pts.)
Composition is neat   _____ (possible 5 pts.)
Grammar and Spelling   _____ (possible 5 pts.)

Essay 2
Demonstrates understanding of the topic   _____ (possible 5 pts.)
Answered the questions completely and accurately   _____ (possible 5 pts.)
Composition is neat   _____ (possible 5 pts.)
Grammar and Spelling   _____ (possible 5 pts.)

Subtotal Points _____ **(possible 55 pts.)**

Extra Credit

Word Puzzle   _____ (5 pt. per completed puzzle)
Complete an Enrichment Activity   _____ (possible 5 pts.)
Oral presentation   _____ (possible 10 pts.)

Total Extra Credit   _____

Total Unit Points _____

GRADE CHART

A   50-55+ points

B   44-49 points

C   38-43 points

D   32-37 points

UNIT 2: MILITARY ROUTES EMERGE

LESSON 4: RAILROADER TUNNELS TO WHITTIER

FACTS TO KNOW

Whittier – A city at the head of the Passage Canal in the U.S. state of Alaska, southeast of Anchorage

Anton Anderson – Engineered the Anton Anderson Tunnel into Whittier

COMPREHENSION QUESTIONS

1) What was the purpose of building a railroad spur from Anchorage to Whittier?

_____

_____

_____

_____

2) Who oversaw the railroad project? What experience did this man have in railroad building? _____

_____

_____

_____

3) What was the tunnel engineer's nickname? Why? What did he consider his greatest accomplishment? _____

_____

_____

_____

4) As the War Department studied possible railroad routes, why did they choose the Passage Canal Line? _____

_____

_____

_____

_____

5) Describe how the Anton Anderson Tunnel was constructed. _____

_____

_____

_____

_____

DISCUSSION QUESTION

(Discuss this question with your teacher or write your answer in essay form below. Use additional paper if necessary.)

What joke did the drilling crew play on Anton Anderson?

_____

_____

_____

_____

_____

_____

_____

_____

_____

_____

_____

_____

_____

_____

_____

_____

ENRICHMENT ACTIVITY

Imagine that you are a news reporter covering the construction of the Anton Anderson Tunnel. Write out a live scene using the information that you learned in Chapter 4.

LEARN MORE

Read more about the Anton Anderson Memorial Tunnel by visiting http://www.tunnel.alaska.gov/history.shtml

UNIT 2: MILITARY ROUTES EMERGE

LESSON 5: ROAD HEADS NORTH TO ALASKA
LESSON 6: OUTPOSTS SPROUT UP

Note: Read both chapters 5 and 6 before completing this lesson.

FACTS TO KNOW

Alaska-Canada Highway – Major highway built to connect Alaska to the Continentual United States and stretched 1,422 miles from Dawson Creek, British Columbia, to Delta Junction, Alaska

Donald MacDonald – Engineer who worked with Clyde Williams to push Congress to build the Alaska-Canada Highway

Clyde "Slim" Williams – Alaska-Canada Highway advocate who traveled the route several times to gain support to build it

COMPREHENSION QUESTIONS

1) What was Donald MacDonald's dream? _____

_____

_____

_____

2) Why did Clyde Williams travel by dog sled to Chicago? _____

_____

_____

_____

3) Why did Clyde Williams go to Washington D.C. after his trip to Chicago?

_____

_____

_____

_____

4) How did Clyde Williams and his friend John Logan become the first men to travel by motorcycle from Alaska to Seattle? _____

_____

_____

_____

_____

5) How did the bombing of Pearl Harbor influence the building of the highway?

_____

_____

_____

_____

6) How did a group of more than 3,000 African-American soldiers who took part in building the Alaska-Canada highway change the perceptions of the time?

_____

_____

_____

_____

7) What kind of conditions did the workers face while building the Alaska-Canada Highway? _____

_____

_____

_____

8) Name three military outposts that you read about in Chapter 6 and one fact about each.

_____

_____

_____

_____

_____

_____

_____

_____

_____

_____

_____

_____

_____

_____

_____

_____

_____

_____

DISCUSSION QUESTION

(Discuss this question with your teacher or write your answer in essay form below. Use additional paper if necessary.)

How did the building of railroads, highways and military outposts change the population of many Alaskan cities?

_____
_____
_____
_____
_____
_____
_____
_____
_____
_____
_____
_____
_____
_____
_____
_____

LEARN MORE

Read more about road transportation in Alaska by visiting http://www.akhistorycourse. org/americas-territory/alaskas-heritage/chapter-4-10-road-transportation

MAP ACTIVITY

Trace the Alaska-Canada Highway on the map below. Mark the major centers that the highway runs through from Dawson Creek in Canada to Delta Junction in Alaska.

1) Fort St. John   2) Fort Nelson   3) Muncho Lake   4) Watson Lake
5) Teslin Lake   6) Whitehorse   7) Tok

UNIT 3: A FEW GOOD MEN

LESSON 7: ESKIMO SCOUTS VOLUNTEER

FACTS TO KNOW

Alaska Territorial Guard – Military unit made up of Native Alaskans to protect the territory from Japanese invaders

U.S. Army Maj. Marvin R. Marston – One of the commanders of the Alaska Territorial Guard who also helped to develop it

Territorial Gov. Ernest Gruening – Authorized the creation of the Alaska Territorial Guard

COMPREHENSION QUESTIONS

1) How did Maj. Marvin Marston get the idea of an Alaska Native defense force?

_____
_____
_____
_____

2) Why was Territorial Gov. Ernest Gruening supportive of the idea when many were not?

_____
_____
_____
_____

3) What reservations did Gov. Gruening have about enlisting Native People into the Alaska Territorial Guard? _____

_____
_____
_____

4) According to Maj. Marston, how could the Native people help protect Alaska?

_____
_____
_____
_____

5) When was the territorial guard disbanded? When was the unit officially recognized as military veterans? _____

_____
_____
_____

DISCUSSION QUESTION

(Discuss this question with your teacher or write your answer in essay form below. Use additional paper if necessary.)

Why do you think the Native people of Alaska were so eager to join the Alaska Territorial Guard?

_____
_____
_____
_____
_____
_____
_____
_____
_____
_____
_____
_____
_____
_____
_____
_____
_____

ENRICHMENT ACTIVITY

Watch this short YouTube video to see some of the faces of people who served in the Alaska Territorial Guard https://www.youtube.com/watch?v=JEU3y5vH_sk

LEARN MORE

Men of the Tundra: Eskimos at War, By Marvin A. Marston. New York: October House, 1969.

This World War II poster depicts the Alaska Territorial Guard

UNIT 3: A FEW GOOD MEN

LESSON 8: THE FLYING BARITONE FROM FAIRBANKS

FACTS TO KNOW

Robert MacArthur Crawford – Composer of the Official U.S. Air Force Song
Composer – A person who writes a song

COMPREHENSION QUESTIONS

1) How did Robert MacArthur Crawford begin his music career in Alaska?

_____

_____

_____

_____

2) At which prestigious U.S. university did Crawford study? What organization did he start while studying there? What did he do upon graduation? _____

_____

_____

_____

3) Besides music, what was Robert MacArthur Crawford's passion? How did he blend his two passions to win a contest? _____

_____

_____

_____

4) What award did he win in 1965 and why? _____

_____

_____

_____

_____

DISCUSSION QUESTION

(Discuss this question with your teacher or write your answer in essay form below. Use additional paper if necessary.)

Why do you think his nickname was the "Flying Baritone"?

_____
_____
_____
_____
_____
_____
_____
_____
_____
_____
_____
_____
_____
_____
_____
_____

ENRICHMENT ACTIVITY

Watch this short YouTube video to hear Robert MacArthur Crawford's famous song:
https://www.youtube.com/watch?v=8B7RzQftARE

LEARN MORE

Read more about John MacArthur Crawford by visiting http://www.militarynews.com/ peninsula-warrior/features/army_features/behind-the-name-crawford-hall-named-for-father-of-the/article_ec5dd9c4-2796-57a0-bce7-6a9865b37a0c.html

UNIT 3: A FEW GOOD MEN

LESSON 9: J. DOOLITTLE: NOME TOWN BOY

FACTS TO KNOW

Jimmy Doolittle – Leader of the famous Doolittle Raiders that bombed Tokyo in 1942
Nome – Gold-rush town located on the southern Seward Peninsula coast on Norton Sound

COMPREHENSION QUESTIONS

1) What was life like for Jimmy Doolittle growing up in Nome in the early 1900s?

_____
_____
_____
_____

2) What lesson did Jimmy Doolittle learn at an early age? What medical condition was he diagnosed with, and what was the cause of it? _____

_____
_____
_____

3) When Jimmy and his mother moved to Los Angeles after his father's death, what did he become known for? _____

_____
_____
_____

4) When did he become interested in aviation? Name some of his accomplishments as an aviator for the military. _____

_____
_____
_____
_____
_____

5) What was the pinnacle of his career? Why was this event important in World War II?

_____
_____
_____
_____

DISCUSSION QUESTION

(Discuss this question with your teacher or write your answer in essay form below. Use additional paper if necessary.)

Do you think that Jimmy Doolittle's childhood experiences prepared him for all the major accomplishments he had as an aviator? Explain your answer.

_____
_____
_____
_____
_____
_____
_____
_____
_____
_____
_____
_____
_____
_____
_____
_____

TIME TO REVIEW

Review Chapters 4-9 of your book before moving on the Unit Review. See how many questions you can answer without looking at your book.

On April 18, 1942, airmen of the U.S. Army Air Forces, led by Lt. Col. James H. (Jimmy) Doolittle, carried the Battle of the Pacific to the heart of the Japanese empire with a surprising and daring raid on military targets at Tokyo, Yokohama, Yokosuka, Nagoya and Kobe. This heroic attack against these major cities was the result of coordination between the Army Air Forces and the U.S. Navy, which carried 16 North American B-25 medium bombers aboard the carrier *USS Hornet* to within take-off distance of the Japanese Islands.

The Japanese thought the airplanes had taken off from a base in the Aleutian Chain of Alaska, which is one reason why they bombed Dutch Harbor, Attu and Kiska in June 1942.

Source: National Museum of the U.S. Air Force

UNIT 2: MILITARY ROUTES EMERGE
UNIT 3: A FEW GOOD MEN

REVIEW LESSONS 4-9

Write down what you remember about:

Whittier _____

_____

Anton Anderson _____

_____

Alaska-Canada Highway _____

_____

Donald MacDonald _____

_____

Clyde "Slim" Williams _____

_____

Alaska Territorial Guard _____

_____

U.S. Army Maj. Marvin R. Marston _____

_____

Territorial Gov. Ernest Gruening _____

_____

Robert MacArthur Crawford _____

_____

Composer _____

_____

Jimmy Doolittle _____

_____

Nome _____

_____

Fill in the blanks:

1) _____ engineered the project that pierced through three miles of solid _____ to open the Port of _____ to the Railbelt and to Fort _____, 75 miles away.

2) The _____ needed a secure transportation system for _____, and a War Department study in 1940 concluded that the _____ Canal line would be safer from enemy attack than the _____ line.

3) Called one of America's greatest _____ projects, the _____ Highway stretched 1,422 miles from _____, _____, to _____, Alaska.

4) In the early 1930s, _____ heard about a Copper Center man who had boasted that he and his _____ could make it to _____ over prospector trails. So _____ contacted _____ and convinced the 50-year-old trapper to prove it.

5) With the bombing of _____ by the _____ on Dec. 7, 1941, the need for more military in Alaska became urgent, and a road to transport _____ became a priority. American officials realized that Alaska was vulnerable to _____ – especially with only 750 miles separating the last island in the _____ Chain and the nearest _____ military base.

6) U.S. Army Maj. _____ conceived the idea of an _____ defense force after visiting _____ Island. While on the island, _____ noted that all the white men, except for a school teacher, had left and that the 700 Natives living in the island's two villages of Savoonga and Gambell were nervous about _____.

7) Territorial Gov. _____ said the response of the _____ men and _____ men differed when asked to join the _____ guard. "In various communities _____ men asked _____," _____ said. "My reply was that they would be _____. They would have the privilege of defending their homes and their families if the enemy should come. No _____ ever raised that question.

8) _____ began his musical career by singing for miners in early _____. His musical _____ ability soon became evident when he wrote the words and music for a song titled "_____."

9) _____ love for _____ and the wild, blue yonder prompted him to enter a contest to find a _____ for the U.S. Army Air Corps. _____, known by now as the "_____," was handed the $1,000 first-place prize at the 1939 National Air races in Cleveland, Ohio.

10) "_____" proclaimed the Nome Nugget headline in April 1942. One of Nome's own, U.S. Army Air Forces pilot Lt. Col. _____, had led the _____ raid in World War _____.

11) With many _____ to his credit, he learned early in life to take care of himself. When he learned that _____ were looked up to in gold-rush Nome, _____ decided to be a _____, since he didn't have any dogs. Years later, doctors diagnosed a _____ deemed caused by over-exertion when he was young.

12) The raid showed the _____ that their homeland was vulnerable to _____ and forced them to withdraw several frontline fighter units from _____ war zones for homeland defense. Their attempt to close the perceived gap in their _____ defense perimeter led directly to the decisive _____ victory during the Battle of Midway in June 1942.

40

The Alaska Territorial Guard, also known as the Eskimo Scouts, played a large role in the protection of Alaska from Japanese forces. Here the Guard marches up Main Street toward St. Michael's Russian Orthodox Church in Sitka in 1944.

World War II Routes & Men
Crossword Puzzle

Read Across and Down clues and fill in blank boxes that match numbers on the clues

Across

6   Alaska governor who authorized the creation of the Alaska Territorial Guard
7   Groups of soldiers
11 Clyde Williams' dogs were part this animal
13 Point in Canada where Alaska-Canada Highway began during WWII
15 Nickname of Clyde Williams
17 Man who led air raid on Tokyo in 1942
20 This Roosevelt said Clyde Williams was "a most vocal advocate" for Alaska Highway
23 Place where military held official ceremony of Alaska Highway completion on Nov. 20, 1942
25 Uninhabited region
26 The man who engineered the railroad tunnel through Maynard Mountain
27 Structures that span rivers and streams
31 Man who wrote and composed the official U.S. Air Force song
32 Alaska Natives signed up to guard Alaska's coasts and became known as this
33 Number of stanzas in the official U.S. Air Force song
34 The practice of keeping White troops and African-American troops separated

Down

1   Man who conceived the idea for an Alaska Native defense force
2   How the military hid the Jesse Lee Home complex in Seward from enemy eyes
3   Alaska's delegate to Congress in 1933
4   Material used to create runways on Alaska islands
5   Pesky insects that suck blood and bothered the workers on the Alaska Highway
8   Only American military aircraft named after a specific person
9   Route that U.S. and Canada chose to build the Alaska-Canada highway in 1942
10 Type of wheels that Clyde Williams put on his sled to mush to Lower 48
11 Port at the end of the railroad spur from Anchorage that military needed for transporting troops and supplies during WWII
12 A powertul tractor with a broad upright blade at the front for clearing ground
14 Military's cold-weather experimental station in Fairbanks
16 Name of Clyde Williams' dog
18 Point in Alaska where Alaska-Canada Highway ended during WWII
19 The nickname for the man who organized the Alaska Natives for the Alaska Territorial Guard
21 Nickname for the Alaska-Canada Highway
22 A person who works for the railroad
24 Means of transportation for William's 1939 trip to Seattle

World War II Routes & Men
Crossword Puzzle

Down (Continued)

28 Town where Clyde Williams mushed for World's Fair in 1933
29 U.S. declared war against this country on Dec. 8, 1941
30 A large woodland

43

UNIT 2: MILITARY ROUTES EMERGE
UNIT 3: A FEW GOOD MEN

UNIT TEST

Choose *three* of the following questions to answer in paragraph form. Use as much detail as possible to completely answer the question. Use extra paper in back of the book if needed.

1) What was the purpose of the Anton Anderson Tunnel? How was it built? Why was this location chosen?

2) Describe the conditions that the construction workers faced building the Alaska-Canada Highway. How did a unit of over 3,000 African-American construction workers change the perceptions of the day?

3) Why did Maj. Marvin Marston think that it would be a good idea to organize an Alaska Native defense force? How did the Native people of Alaska react to the invitation to join the unit? Why?

4) Who was the "Flying Baritone"? How did he begin his musical career? What song was he most famous for? Why was this song so popular?

5) How did Jimmy Doolittle's childhood impact his career as an adult? What were some of his accomplishments? How did his most famous accomplishment change World War II?

_____
_____
_____
_____
_____
_____
_____
_____
_____
_____
_____
_____
_____

UNIT 2: MILITARY ROUTES EMERGE
UNIT 3: A FEW GOOD MEN

Review Questions   _____ (possible 12 pts.)
Fill-the-Blanks   _____ (possible 12 pts.)

Unit Test

Essay 1

Demonstrates understanding of the topic   _____ (possible 5 pts.)
Answered the questions completely and accurately   _____ (possible 5 pts.)
Composition is neat   _____ (possible 5 pts.)
Grammar and Spelling   _____ (possible 5 pts.)

Essay 2

Demonstrates understanding of the topic   _____ (possible 5 pts.)
Answered the questions completely and accurately   _____ (possible 5 pts.)
Composition is neat   _____ (possible 5 pts.)
Grammar and Spelling   _____ (possible 5 pts.)

Essay 3

Demonstrates understanding of the topic   _____ (possible 5 pts.)
Answered the questions completely and accurately   _____ (possible 5 pts.)
Composition is neat   _____ (possible 5 pts.)
Grammar and Spelling   _____ (possible 5 pts.)

Subtotal Points _____ **(possible 84 pts.)**

Extra Credit

Word Puzzle   _____ (5 pt. per completed puzzle)
Complete an Enrichment Activity   _____ (possible 5 pts.)
Oral presentation   _____ (possible 10 pts.)

Total Extra Credit   _____

Total Unit Points _____

GRADE CHART

A   76-84+ points

B   67-74 points

C   59-66 points

D   51-58 points

UNIT 4: CONFLICT IN THE ALEUTIANS

LESSON 10: DUTCH HARBOR ATTACKED

FACTS TO KNOW

Dutch Harbor – Area on Unalaska Island that was attacked by Japanese troops in 1942

Japanese Zeros – Fighter aircraft also known as Mitsubishi A6M or Navy Type 0

Code breakers – Military personnel trained to interpret encrypted messages

COMPREHENSION QUESTIONS

1) What happened during the two-day attack on Dutch Harbor in 1942? _____

_____

_____

_____

2) How many Americans died in the attack? Explain how it could have been worse.

_____

_____

_____

3) What misconceptions did the Japanese planners have about American military support in the region? _____

_____

_____

_____

4) How did code breakers help American soldiers learn about the Japanese plan of attack?

_____

_____

_____

_____

5) How did American soldiers respond to these plans? _____
_____
_____
_____

DISCUSSION QUESTION

(Discuss this question with your teacher or write your answer in essay form below. Use additional paper if necessary.)

Do you think that attack on Dutch Harbor changed Alaska? Explain your answer.

_____
_____
_____
_____
_____
_____
_____
_____
_____
_____
_____
_____
_____
_____
_____
_____
_____
_____

ENRICHMENT ACTIVITY

The attack on Dutch Harbor was big news in Alaska in 1942. Imagine that you are a newspaper journalist putting together a front-page story breaking the news on the attack. What would your headline read? What picture would you use? What would the caption be for that photo?

LEARN MORE

Read more about the attack on Dutch Harbor by visiting
http://www.sitnews.us/0612News/060112/060112_dutch_harbor.html

UNIT 4: CONFLICT IN THE ALEUTIANS

LESSON 11: ENEMY INVADES ATTU

FACTS TO KNOW

Kiska – Island in the Aleutian Chain that Japanese soldiers occupied in June 1942

Charles Foster Jones – 60-year-old radio technician who operated a government radio and weather-reporting station who was captured and killed by Japanese soldiers during the attack on Attu

Etta Jones – Bureau of Indian Affairs teacher who was captured by Japanese soldiers during the attack on Attu and sent to a concentration camp in Japan

COMPREHENSION QUESTIONS

1) What happened two days after the attack on Dutch Harbor on June 6, 1942?

_____
_____
_____
_____
_____

2) Explain why the terrain and weather was challenging for both Japanese and American military forces during World War II? _____

_____
_____
_____
_____

3) What did the Japanese soldiers do to the Aleut people and Etta and Charles Jones?

_____
_____
_____
_____
_____

4) What were the Aleuts' living conditions like in Japan? _____

_____

_____

_____

5) How did half of the Alaska Native prisoners die? What did the Japanese soldiers do with the remaining prisoners? _____

_____

_____

_____

DISCUSSION QUESTION

(Discuss this question with your teacher or write your answer in essay form below. Use additional paper if necessary.)

Why did Japan attack Attu and Kiska?

_____

_____

_____

_____

_____

_____

_____

_____

_____

_____

_____

_____

_____

_____

_____

_____

_____

LEARN MORE

Look for this article at your local library:
"The Aleutians," Alaska Geographic Society, Vol. 7, No. 3, 1980.

MAP ACTIVITY

Locate the follow places from your reading on the map below:

      1) Mainland Alaska   2) Russia   3) Japan   4) Bering Sea

      5) Unalaska   6) Dutch Harbor   7) Attu   8) Kiska

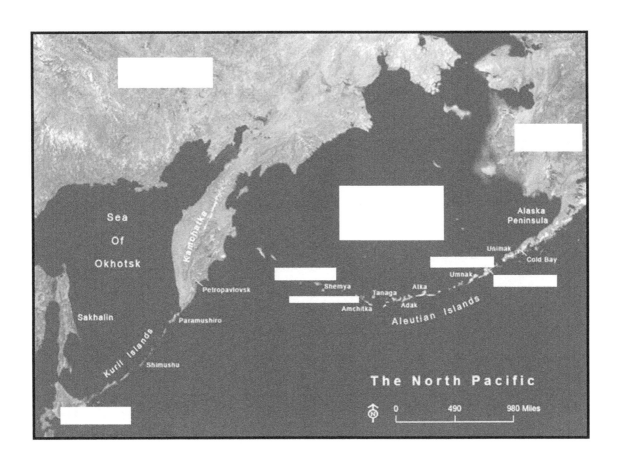

UNIT 4: CONFLICT IN THE ALEUTIANS

LESSON 12: JAPANESE AMERICANS INTERRED

FACTS TO KNOW

Internment – Forced relocation or imprisonment of people who are often seen as a threat

Executive order – Policy signed by the U.S. President that directs the federal government to do something

Minidoka Relocation Center – One of 10 internment camps for Japanese Americans in the U.S.

COMPREHENSION QUESTIONS

1) What was the purpose of Executive Order 9066 signed by U.S. President Franklin D. Roosevelt? _____

_____

_____

_____

2) Describe the conditions at Minidoka Relocation Center. What was the detainees reaction when they arrived? _____

_____

_____

_____

3) Why did many people become sick at the internment camp? _____

_____

_____

_____

4) How many detainees were American citizens? How long were they detained?

_____

_____

_____

5) What did President Roosevelt's Secretary of the Interior later say about the internment camps? _____

_____

_____

DISCUSSION QUESTION

(Discuss this question with your teacher or write your answer in essay form below. Use additional paper if necessary.)

How many people were convicted of spying for Japan during the war and where were they from?

_____

_____

_____

_____

_____

_____

_____

_____

_____

_____

_____

_____

_____

_____

_____

_____

ENRICHMENT ACTIVITY

Visit the link below and read 2-3 personal accounts of individuals that were placed in internment camps. Write a short summary of what you learned about what life was like for those that were forced to live in these camps.

https://www.afsc.org/document/afsc-oral-history-project-japanese-american-internment (look for the PDF link at the bottom of the page)

LEARN MORE

Read more about the Japanese internment camps by visiting http://www.pbs.org/childofcamp/history/timeline.html

UNIT 4: CONFLICT IN THE ALEUTIANS

LESSON 13: ALEUTS BECOME REFUGEES

FACTS TO KNOW

Aleuts – Native Alaskans from the Aleutian Islands who also call themselves Unangan
Pribilof Islands – A group of volcanic islands off the coast of mainland Alaska
that formerly were called Northern Fur Seal Islands

COMPREHENSION QUESTIONS

1) After the Japanese bombed _____, occupied _____ and invaded
_____ in June 1942, the U.S. military ordered a hasty _____ of more than
800 _____ living in the Aleutian and _____ islands.

2) Who did the sailors find when they came ashore at Atka? Why were they the only
people there? _____
_____
_____
_____

3) How did Daniel C.R. Benson describe the orders that the sailors were given?
_____
_____
_____
_____

4) Where were the Aleuts taken? _____
_____
_____
_____

5) Describe some of the conditions at the duration villages. _____
_____
_____
_____
_____

6) Why did the Aleut people hate the area that the miltary brought them to be safe?

_____

_____

_____

_____

DISCUSSION QUESTION

(Discuss this question with your teacher or write your answer in essay form below. Use additional paper if necessary.)

In what major industry were the Aleuts forced to work in the Pribilof Islands?

_____

_____

_____

_____

_____

_____

_____

_____

_____

_____

_____

_____

_____

_____

_____

_____

ENRICHMENT ACTIVITY

What similarities and differences do you see between the internment of Japanese Americans and the Aleuts during World War II? Write at least two paragraphs to compare and contrast these two events in history.

LEARN MORE

The Treatment of the Aleuts: A World War II Tragedy. Anchorage, Alaska: The Aleutian/ Pribilof Islands Association

UNIT 4: CONFLICT IN THE ALEUTIANS

LESSON 14: ENEMY OUSTED FROM ALEUTIANS

FACTS TO KNOW

Attu – 40-mile island on the westernmost tip of the Aleutians where the U.S. military made its first-ever amphibious landing

Massacre Bay – One of the landing points where U.S. troops attacked Japanese soldiers

COMPREHENSION QUESTIONS

1) Why did the U.S. military send 15,000 troops to Attu in May 1943? _____

_____

_____

_____

2) What happened when the troops got to Massacre Bay? _____

_____

_____

_____

3) How long was the battle expected to last? How long did it last? How many American soldiers lost their lives? _____

_____

_____

_____

_____

4) What did many Japanese soldiers do to prevent being captured by U.S. soldiers?

_____

_____

_____

_____

5) What happened during the invasion of Kiska in 1943? _____

_____

_____

_____

_____

DISCUSSION QUESTION

(Discuss this question with your teacher or write your answer in essay form below. Use additional paper if necessary.)

Thousands of soldiers lost their lives during World War II. What are some ways that we can remember those that lost their lives during war?

_____

_____

_____

_____

_____

_____

_____

_____

_____

_____

_____

_____

_____

_____

_____

_____

TIME TO REVIEW

Review Chapters 10-14 of your book before moving on the Unit Review. See how many questions you can answer without looking at your book.

UNIT 4: CONFLICT IN THE ALEUTIANS

REVIEW LESSONS 10-14

Write down what you remember about:

Dutch Harbor _____
_____

Japanese Zeros _____
_____

Code breakers _____
_____

Kiska _____
_____

Charles Foster Jones _____
_____

Etta Jones _____
_____

Internment _____
_____

Executive order _____
_____

Minidoka Relocation Center _____
_____

Aleuts _____
_____

Pribilof Islands _____
_____

Attu _____
_____

Massacre Bay _____
_____

Fill in the blanks:

1) _____ troops invaded the _____ Islands in June _____. During the two-day attack, _____ U.S. soldiers and sailors, as well as 10 civilians, died. But the devastation at _____ Harbor could have been worse. Rear Adm. Kakuji Kakuta had dispatched more than _____ from two small aircraft carriers. Due to _____, less than half the planes reached the islands.

2) American _____ learned in mid-March that the _____ planned to bomb, and then _____, the _____.

3) On June _____, two days after the attack on _____ Harbor, a Japanese special landing party and 500 troops came ashore at _____ around 10:30 p.m.

4) The Japanese kept the _____ fishermen busy for three days supplying the troops with food. Then the villagers were told to grab some _____ for themselves, because they were _____. They were kept in the unpleasant-smelling hold of a ship for the weeklong _____, never seeing daylight until they reached _____.

5) The _____ Islands are _____ or swampy muskeg. Attu has high _____ terrain, rising 3,000 feet, starting close to its shoreline and stretching into the interior of the island. It usually has a cold, damp _____ accompanied by _____.

6) _____ signed Executive Order 9066 in February 1942. It ordered the _____ of more than 112,000 _____ from the West Coast. Those with _____ ancestry were taken from their homes, businesses and schools and put in _____.

7) U.S. authorities evacuated hundreds of men, women and children from the _____ and _____ islands following the Japanese attacks on _____. These people were relocated to "_____" in Southeast Alaska.

8) For most of the camps, _____ for the children and _____ with the outside world was sparse. The evacuees lacked _____ _____.

9) In May _____, Americans finally dislodged the enemy from its toehold on the _____ tip of the _____. They did it in a battle that became – in proportion to the number of opposing troops – the second most _____ in the Pacific, second only to Iwo Jima.

10) It was a tricky campaign; the _____ was almost as hard to conquer as the enemy, and the _____ took their toll as well as the enemy bullets. By the seventh day of battle, _____ had suffered 1,100 casualties, 500 of them from exposure. Before the battle was over, there would be 549 _____ and 2,351 _____ dead.

11) On Aug. 15, 1943, the Allied invasion of _____ began. But there was no _____ to the 32,000 U.S. and Canadian forces because no _____ troops were left on the island. Under _____, the _____ fleet had secretly removed its 5,000 soldiers from _____ by I-class submarines and surface vessels prior to the Allied attack.

Japanese Attack Aleutians
Word Search Puzzle
Find the words listed below

```
A U N A G A N B B O F L B O Y Y Y F N
S F U U F O R T M E A R S F Y P A W E A
Z D B Q T O X O M Z W X A W J F B F A T
I O K H P Y A B R E T N U F K O D N S U
F N Q M Y A B E R C A S S A M X L E M K
S R E I D L O S H O L T Z B A Y O U F A
U S G P Q O T O M A M A Y V Q K C V Z J
N E J S D N A L S I F O L I B I R P X G
A N E P S E G A L L I V N O I T A R U D
L O O D G R V K L P L I F M B S D I D X
A J C O J S L A A E I A A F F M E A U S
S A R N N M W N C C U L X O R I O L T O
K T F A B S W M Y U L T G V B N U E C R
A T S G T B I U K I A H S O R I B U H E
C E F O R T G L E N N T M M G D U T H Z
L D G H M L U S L Y R B I A B O P I A R
G Y T N J P R T O I E U L O O K R A R Q
V A N Z A K S I K R K U F K N A X N B J
K N W O I R E T S W P N Q O P M A S O O
G X P F L S J R E D B E A C H Q P O R K
```

DUTCH HARBOR	UNALASKA	ATTU	FUNTER BAY	AKUTAN
KISKA	FORT MEARS	ZEROS	EVACUATION	RED BEACH
BOMBERS	ALEUTIANS	YAMAMOTO	MASSACRE BAY	ALLIES
FORT GLENN	UMNAK	COLD BAY	UNANGAN	
ETTA JONES	ALEUTS	MINIDOKA	HOLTZ BAY	
DURATION VILLAGES	PRIBILOF ISLANDS	KILLISNOO	SOLDIERS	

UNIT 4: CONFLICT IN THE ALEUTIANS

UNIT TEST

Choose *three* of the following questions to answer in paragraph form. Use as much detail as possible to completely answer the question. Use extra paper in back of the book if needed.

1) Describe the attack at Dutch Harbor. How could it have been worse?

2) What did the Japanese do with the Aleuts at Kiska?

3) Why was the Aleutian Chain a difficult place for both U.S. and Japanese soldiers to battle?

4) What similarities and differences do you see between the internment of Japanese Americans and the Aleuts during World War II?

5) Why did the United States send 15,000 troops to the island of Attu in 1943? Describe the battle.

_____

_____

_____

_____

_____

_____

_____

_____

_____

_____

_____

_____

_____

_____

_____

_____

_____

_____

_____

UNIT 4: CONFLICT IN THE ALEUTIANS

Review Questions _____ (possible 13 pts.)
Fill-the-Blanks _____ (possible 11 pts.)

Unit Test
Essay 1
Demonstrates understanding of the topic _____ (possible 5 pts.)
Answered the questions completely and accurately _____ (possible 5 pts.)
Composition is neat _____ (possible 5 pts.)
Grammar and Spelling _____ (possible 5 pts.)

Essay 2
Demonstrates understanding of the topic _____ (possible 5 pts.)
Answered the questions completely and accurately _____ (possible 5 pts.)
Composition is neat _____ (possible 5 pts.)
Grammar and Spelling _____ (possible 5 pts.)

Essay 3
Demonstrates understanding of the topic _____ (possible 5 pts.)
Answered the questions completely and accurately _____ (possible 5 pts.)
Composition is neat _____ (possible 5 pts.)
Grammar and Spelling _____ (possible 5 pts.)

Subtotal Points _____ **(possible 84 pts.)**

Extra Credit
Word Puzzle _____ (5 pt. per completed puzzle)
Complete an Enrichment Activity _____ (possible 5 pts.)
Oral presentation _____ (possible 10 pts.)

Total Extra Credit _____

Total Unit Points _____

GRADE CHART

A 76-84+ points

B 67-74 points

C 59-66 points

D 51-58 points

UNIT 5: 1940s POSTWAR NEWS

LESSON 15: 1945: DISCRIMINATION TORPEDOED

FACTS TO KNOW

Segregation – Process of separating people of different races or religions from each other

Alberta Schenck – Civil rights activist for Native rights who was discriminated against in a Nome theater

The 1867 Treaty of Cessions – Declared Alaska Natives were not deemed U.S. citizens because they were "uncivilized"

COMPREHENSION QUESTIONS

1) Describe the segregation that Alaska Natives were subjected to in the 1900s. What other race experienced similar discrimination in the United States? _____

_____

_____

_____

2) What event in Nome brought a spotlight on the discrimination against Alaska Natives?

_____

_____

_____

_____

3) How did Maj. Marston get involved in this case? What was the result?

_____

_____

_____

_____

4) Who were the Alaska Native Brotherhood and Sisterhood? What injustices did they fight? _____

_____

_____

_____

5) Why do Alaskan's celebrate Elizabeth Peratrovich Day? _____

_____

_____

_____

DISCUSSION QUESTION

(Discuss this question with your teacher or write your answer in essay form below. Use additional paper if necessary.)

How do you think segregation affects a society?

_____

_____

_____

_____

_____

_____

_____

_____

_____

_____

_____

_____

_____

_____

_____

_____

ENRICHMENT ACTIVITY

Choose one article from the link below to read more about segregation in Alaska. Take notes about what you are reading, and prepare a 2-3-minute oral report about what you read.

LEARN MORE

Read more about segregation in Alaska by visiting
http://www.alaskool.org/projects/JimCrow/Jimcrow.htm

UNIT 5: 1940s POSTWAR NEWS

LESSON 16: 1947: REEVE AIRWAYS TAKES FLIGHT

FACTS TO KNOW

Robert "Bob" Campbell Reeve – Bush pilot who started Reeve Airways
Reeve Aleutian Airways – Airline that served the Aleutian Chain

COMPREHENSION QUESTIONS

1) Why was Robert Reeve's nickname "Glacier Pilot"? _____

_____

_____

_____

2) How did Robert Reeve fall in love with flying? How did he get to Alaska?

_____

_____

_____

_____

3) What event in 1937 caused him to stop glacier landings? _____

_____

_____

_____

4) How did Robert Reeve start Reeve Aleutian Airways? _____

_____

_____

_____

DISCUSSION QUESTION

(Discuss this question with your teacher or write your answer in essay form below. Use additional paper if necessary.)

What can we learn from Robert Reeve's story of going from a poor young stowaway, to a distinguished bush pilot and the owner of an airline?

_____
_____
_____
_____
_____
_____
_____
_____
_____
_____
_____
_____
_____
_____
_____
_____
_____

ENRICHMENT ACTIVITY

Read more about Robert Reeve on the National Aviation Hall of Fame Website using the link below. See if you can find one other inductee on the Website that you read about in your textbook: http://www.nationalaviation.org/our-enshrinees/reeve-robert/

LEARN MORE

Look for this book at your local library:
Glacier Pilot. Beth Day. Garden City, New Jersey: 1974.

UNIT 5: 1940s POSTWAR NEWS

LESSON 17: 1948: MURDERER NOMINATED KING

FACTS TO KNOW

Anchorage Fur Rendezvous – Annual winter festival in Anchorage
Jacob Marunenko – Also known as "Jack Marchin" or "Russian Jack"

COMPREHENSION QUESTIONS

1) What are some of the events that occurred in Anchorage during the 1920s and 1930s?

_____
_____
_____
_____

2) Where was Jacob Marunenko from? How did he earn a living in Alaska?

_____
_____
_____
_____

3) Summarize his account of events on March 22, 1937? _____

_____
_____
_____
_____

4) What was the result of the case against him for this incident? _____

_____
_____
_____
_____

5) What honor did "Russian Jack" receive during the Anchorage Fur Rendezvous?

_____
_____
_____
_____

DISCUSSION QUESTION

(Discuss this question with your teacher or write your answer in essay form below. Use additional paper if necessary.)

Can you name another person in history whose past crimes did not stop them from being honored later in life for the good things that they did?

_____
_____
_____
_____
_____
_____
_____
_____
_____
_____
_____
_____
_____
_____
_____
_____
_____

ENRICHMENT ACTIVITY

Creatively narrate the story of Russian Jack by either writing a poem, drawing a picture, making a storyboard, etc. Share your narration with the class.

LEARN MORE

Read more about Russian Jack by visiting
http://www.alaskahistory.org/biographies/marunenko-jacob-russian-jack/

UNIT 5: 1940s POSTWAR NEWS

LESSON 18: 1948: ALASKA AIRLINES MAKES HISTORY

FACTS TO KNOW

Alaska Airlines – Famous airline that began as McGee Airlines in 1932
Linious "Mac" McGee – Fur trader who started Alaska Airlines
Berlin Airlift – Airlines delivered much needed supplies to Berlin after the Soviet
  Union blocked all rail and road access to the German city

COMPREHENSION QUESTIONS

1) Describe how Linious McGee and Harvey Barnhill started the airline. _____
_____
_____
_____
_____

2) What concept did Linious McGee pioneer as he purchased more airplanes for the
airline? _____
_____
_____
_____

3) When did the airline become Alaska Airlines? _____
_____
_____
_____

4) How did Alaska Airlines help the city of Berlin? _____
_____
_____
_____

5) What was Operation Magic Carpet? How did Alaska Airlines get involved?

_____
_____
_____
_____
_____

DISCUSSION QUESTION

(Discuss this question with your teacher or write your answer in essay form below. Use additional paper if necessary.)

How did involvement in the Berlin Airlift and Operation Magic Carpet benefit Alaska Airlines (other than monetarily)?

_____
_____
_____
_____
_____
_____
_____
_____
_____
_____
_____
_____
_____
_____
_____
_____

ENRICHMENT ACTIVITY

Using the information that you read in Chapter 18, create a timeline of events for Alaska Airlines beginning at the founding of McGee Airlines.

LEARN MORE

Read more about Alaska Airlines involvement with Operation Magic Carpet by reading https://www.alaskaair.com/content/about-us/history/magic-carpet.aspx

UNIT 5: 1940s POSTWAR NEWS

LESSON 19: IN OTHER NEWS ...

COMPREHENSION QUESTIONS

Write one or two sentences about each of the following events:

1) **1940: Sydney Laurence Dies** _____
_____
_____

2) **1943: Venetie Reservation Created** _____
_____
_____

3) **1944: Alaska-Juneau Gold Mine Shuts Down** _____
_____
_____

4) **1945: Floating Clinics Take to Alaska Waters** _____
_____
_____

5) **1947: Kake Becomes First Incorporated School District** _____
_____
_____

6) **1947: Southeast Natives File Land Claims Suit** _____
_____
_____

TIME TO REVIEW

Review Chapters 15-19 of your book before moving on the Unit Review. See how many questions you can answer without looking at your book.

UNIT 5: 1940s POSTWAR NEWS

REVIEW LESSONS 15-19

Write down what you remember about:

Segregation _____

_____

Alberta Schenck _____

_____

The 1867 Treaty of Cessions _____

_____

Robert "Bob" Campbell Reeve _____

_____

Reeve Aleutian Airways _____

_____

Anchorage Fur Rendezvous _____

_____

Jacob Marunenko _____

_____

Alaska Airlines _____

_____

Linious "Mac" McGee _____

_____

Berlin Airlift _____

_____

Fill in the blanks:

1) Even though Alaska's _____ served with distinction guarding Alaska's borders, _____ thrived throughout the territory. Just like _____ in many of the contiguous United States, _____ had separate _____ _____ than whites in public areas.

2) _____ had bucked the long-held status quo and dared to sit in the _____ section of the theater. She wrote about the injustices directed toward _____ in an essay for her high school history class. It was published in The _____ Nugget newspaper.

3) _____, an Alaska Native, was instrumental in the passage of the Anti-_____ Act in _____. Then the _____ case of 1976 ended more _____ by allowing schools to be built in _____ communities.

4) One of Alaska's most respected _____ launched his own _____ with a 21-passenger Douglas DC-3 C-47 Skytrain Dakota purchased from the U.S. Air Force in March 1947. _____ birthed _____ to serve the people of the Aleutian Chain.

5) _____ pioneered new flight routes to get to hard-to-reach _____, developed a method for landing on mud flats with skis and set down on many _____. His 2,000-some _____ landings earned him the nickname "_____."

6) In 1948, one of Anchorage's most colorful characters, _____, was nominated for _____ during the Anchorage _____. Known as _____, this homesteader also was a _____.

7) In his account of events during his trial, _____ explained that he shot _____ while being choked. "_____" admitted firing the shot that killed _____ instantly. But he testified that _____ of killing the man.

8) Alaska Airlines flew into the history books when, in 1948, it participated in the _____. Manager _____ efforts landed the company a lucrative deal during the _____ to ferry tons of _____ into _____ after the Soviet Union blocked all rail and road access to the German city.

9) _____ carried up to 150 people per trip during Operation _____. The government of _____, established in 1947 when the United Nations passed a resolution to partition _____, mounted airlift operations in 1949 to bring _____ people to the new country after the Imam of Yemen agreed to let 45,000 _____ leave his country.

1940s People of Influence
Word Scramble Puzzle
Unscramble the words below

1. alarbet cnecshk

   Bucked the status quo and sat in the "white only" section of Nome movie theater

2. wmiilal ulpa

   First Alaska Native to serve in the Alaska Territorial Legislature

3. thibeaezl vrpcoihrate

   Alaska Native woman who was instrumental in passage of Anti-Discrimination Bill in 1945

4. brrote veree

   Started an airline to serve the Aleutian Chain and was known as the Glacier Pilot

5. rnisuas jkac

   Anchorage character who murdered a man and still became the Mardi Gras King of the Anchorage Fur Rendezvous

6. uionlis cgeme

   Acknowledged founder of Alaska Airlines

7. terorb sllie

   Started an airlines in Ketchikan in 1936

8. ikkr rtipcrikak

   Began Cordova Airlines in 1934

9. dnyeys eacrnleu

   Legendary Alaska artist known for dramatic landscape paintings

10. restne ggiernnu

   Territorial governor who signed Anti-Discrimination Bill into law in 1945

UNIT 5: 1940s POSTWAR NEWS

UNIT TEST

Choose *two* of the following questions to answer in paragraph form. Use as much detail as possible to completely answer the question. Use extra paper in back of the book if needed.

1) Describe segregation and discrimination that Alaska Natives experienced in the 1900s.

2) How did Robert Reeve start Reeve Airways? What else was he famous for?

3) Who was Russian Jack? Describe the events that led to his conviction in 1937.

4) What are some ways that Alaska Airlines made history? Explain at least one of these events in detail.

5) Describe at least two other important events in Alaska history that you read about in this unit and have not written about in this test.

_____

_____

_____

_____

_____

_____

_____

_____

_____

_____

_____

_____

_____

_____

_____

_____

_____

_____

_____

_____

_____

_____

_____

UNIT 5: 1940s POSTWAR NEWS

Review Questions _____ (possible 10 pts.)
Fill-the-Blanks _____ (possible 9 pts.)

Unit Test
Essay 1
Demonstrates understanding of the topic _____ (possible 5 pts.)
Answered the questions completely and accurately _____ (possible 5 pts.)
Composition is neat _____ (possible 5 pts.)
Grammar and Spelling _____ (possible 5 pts.)

Essay 2
Demonstrates understanding of the topic _____ (possible 5 pts.)
Answered the questions completely and accurately _____ (possible 5 pts.)
Composition is neat _____ (possible 5 pts.)
Grammar and Spelling _____ (possible 5 pts.)

Subtotal Points _____ **(possible 59 pts.)**

Extra Credit
Word Puzzle _____ (5 pt. per completed puzzle)
Complete an Enrichment Activity _____ (possible 5 pts.)
Oral presentation _____ (possible 10 pts.)

Total Extra Credit _____

Total Unit Points _____

GRADE CHART

A   54-59+ points

B   48-53 points

C   42-47 points

D   36-41 points

UNIT 6: COLD WAR ERA

LESSON 20: 'RED SCARE' BRINGS BOOM

FACTS TO KNOW

Union of Soviet Socialist Republics –Rival of the United States with nuclear power
Distant Early Warning System – Radar network designed to warn Alaska of nuclear attack

COMPREHENSION QUESTIONS

1) What was the "red scare"? _____

_____

_____

_____

2) Why did Alaska become the "eyes" of the nation in the 1940s? _____

_____

_____

_____

_____

3) How did military spending in the 1950s connect Alaska's communities? _____

_____

_____

_____

_____

_____

4) How did the Alaska Railroad benefit from military spending? _____

_____

_____

_____

_____

_____

5) How did the Alaska road system benefit from military spending? _____

_____
_____
_____
_____

DISCUSSION QUESTION

(Discuss this question with your teacher or write your answer in essay form below. Use additional paper if necessary.)

How did increased military presence in the 1950s affect Alaska's economy?

_____
_____
_____
_____
_____
_____
_____
_____
_____
_____
_____
_____
_____
_____
_____
_____

ENRICHMENT ACTIVITY

Imagine that you are living in Alaska in the 1950s and experiencing all the changes to your community (improved communication, transportation, etc.). Write a short story or diary entry about your experience.

LEARN MORE

The Opening of Alaska. William L. "Billy" Mitchell. Edited by Lyman L. Woodman. Anchorage: Cook Inlet Historical Society, 1982.

UNIT 6: COLD WAR ERA

LESSON 21: ANCHORAGE: JEWEL ON THE TUNDRA

FACTS TO KNOW

Anchorage Light and Power Co. –Anchorage power company had to increase production for the fast-increasing population

Tundra – A vast, flat, treeless region in which the subsoil is permanently frozen

COMPREHENSION QUESTIONS

1) Why did people pour into Anchorage in the 1950s? _____

_____

_____

_____

2) What problems did the large increase in population cause? _____

_____

_____

_____

_____

3) How did the people of Anchorage trick U.S. Postmaster General James A. Farley into recommending the building of the Old Federal Building? _____

_____

_____

_____

_____

4) According to Clifford Cernick, how were the average statesider's conception of Anchorage challenged with all of the changes to the city? _____

_____

_____

_____

_____

5) Why was Anchorage the first city outside of the contiguous 48 states to be named an "All-America City"? _____

_____
_____
_____
_____

DISCUSSION QUESTION

(Discuss this question with your teacher or write your answer in essay form below. Use additional paper if necessary.)

What were the typical prices for a meal in Anchorage in 1950? How does this compare to prices today?

_____
_____
_____
_____
_____
_____
_____
_____
_____
_____
_____
_____
_____
_____
_____
_____

ENRICHMENT ACTIVITY

Imagine that you are a journalist for a national newspaper. Write a short newspaper story covering Anchorage being named All-America City in 1956. Include several reasons for why the city received this honor.

LEARN MORE

Anchorage: All American City. Evangeline Atwood. Binfords and Mort. 1957

UNIT 6: COLD WAR ERA

LESSON 22: OTHER ALASKA TOWNS GROW

COMPREHENSION QUESTIONS

Write one to two sentences about how each city benefited from defense spending during the 1950s.

1) Fairbanks _____
_____
_____

2) Nome _____
_____
_____

3) Seward _____
_____
_____

4) Valdez _____
_____
_____

5) Kodiak _____
_____
_____

6) Sitka _____
_____
_____

7) Skagway _____
_____
_____

MAP ACTIVITY

Locate each of the cities listed on Page 80 on the map below:

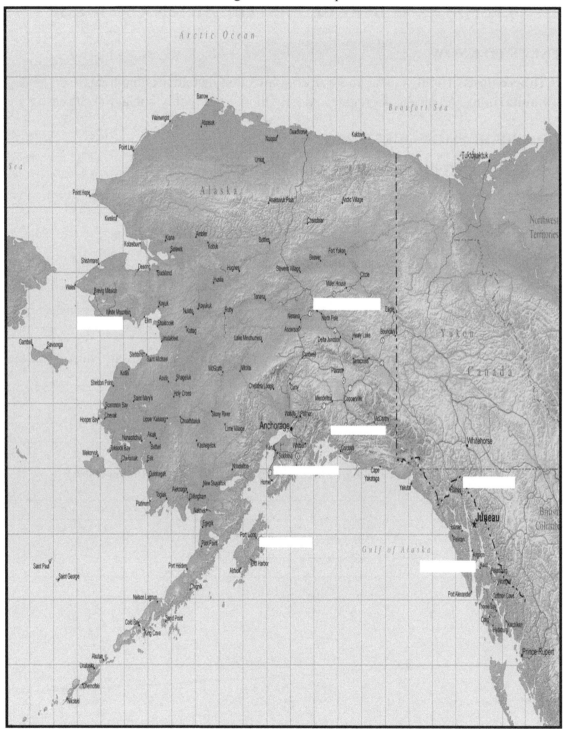

UNIT 6: COLD WAR ERA

LESSON 23: TUBERCULOSIS: THE ALASKA SCOURGE

FACTS TO KNOW

Tuberculosis –Highly contagious bacterial infection that attacks the lungs
Sanitarium – A place to segregate and treat those with highly contagious diseases

COMPREHENSION QUESTIONS

1) Why was tuberculosis especially dangerous for Native Alaskans? _____

_____

_____

_____

2) When was Alaska's first sanatorium opened? What was it like? _____

_____

_____

_____

3) How did Gov. Ernest Gruening help fight the tuberculosis crisis in Native Alaskan villages? _____

_____

_____

_____

4) How did the government finally make a difference in the tuberculosis crisis?

_____

_____

_____

_____

DISCUSSION QUESTION

(Discuss this question with your teacher or write your answer in essay form below. Use additional paper if necessary.)

How was health care different for white Alaskans and Native Alaskans in the 1950s?

_____
_____
_____
_____
_____
_____
_____
_____
_____
_____
_____
_____
_____
_____
_____

TIME TO REVIEW

Review Chapters 20-23 of your book before moving on the Unit Review. See how many questions you can answer without looking at your book.

Cold War Era
Crossword Puzzle

Read Across and Down clues and fill in blank boxes that match numbers on the clues

Across

1   Name of project that solved power problems in Anchorage area in 1950s
4   Electric cooperative that formed in 1950s in the Anchorage area
10 This disease, called the Alaska Scourge, ravaged Alaska Native villages during the 1940-50s
11 Resort built near Girdwood in 1954
15 An airline pilot compared Anchorage to this international city
20 Military dollars spent to improve this road that connected Valdez to Fairbanks helped Valdez' fishing community
21 Anchorage residents fooled a U.S. official in order to get this new government building built in 1930s
22 This is what Alaska children nicknamed floating clinics like the *M/V Hygiene*
24 Fairbanks dairy that had to close its doors when cheaper products and more variety began arriving in Alaska via the Alaska-Canada Highway
21 Anchorage's first television station that began broadcasting in 1953
28 By 1952, this was the fastest-growing city in North America
31 This highway that connects Resurrection Bay to Anchorage was completed in 1951
33 A vast, flat, treeless region in which the subsoil is permanently frozen
34 The nuns of this order built a new 52-bed hospital at Ninth Avenue and L Street in Anchorage in 1939

Down

1   Russian Jack remembered hunting this animal in what became downtown Anchorage
2   The U.S. military built a naval base on this island near Sitka
3   Code name for Alaska Integrated Communications Enterprise
5   People thought this Russian leader wanted to take over the world
6   Daily passenger service between Anchorage and Fairbanks began on June 18, 1951
8   The device that the USSR developed that frightened the world in late-1940s
9   Only six of 30 first-graders that contracted TB lived to finish out the 1941 school year in this northern village
11 Man behind Anchorage's first television station that began broadcasting in 1953
12 Air Force station near Nenana
13 The addition of a canal to connect Lake Hood and Lake Spenard made this waterway the world's largest base for these types of aircraft
14 Fear that gripped the nation following World War II when USSR became a rival was known as this
16 Wrecked ocean-going tanker that was used to provide about half the electricity needed for Anchorage during 1930s
11 One Southwest Alaska base that was reactivated in the 1950s to intercept Russian aircraft foraying into U.S. airspace

Cold War Era
Crossword Puzzle

18 Russian satellite launched in 1951
19 Anchorage radio station that went on the air in 1948
23 Alaska's first TB sanatorium was built near this Southeast town
25 New U.S. Air Force base built near Fairbanks during Cold War era
26 Fairbanks Air Force base
29 Anchorage Air Force base
30 Early warning system used this type of detection
32 This community became home to a chief U.S. Navy base during 1950s and quadrupled its population

UNIT 6: COLD WAR ERA

REVIEW LESSONS 20-23

Write down what you remember about:

Union of Soviet Socialist Republics _____

_____

Distant Early Warning System _____

_____

Anchorage Light and Power Co. _____

_____

Tundra _____

_____

Tuberculosis _____

_____

Sanitarium _____

_____

Fill in the blanks:

1) "_____" gripped the nation following World War II. The Union of _____, an ally during the war, became an international rival armed with _____ after it exploded its first _____ and built an intercontinental bomber in late 1949. And Alaska, offering the shortest route for a Soviet _____ on America, became the "_____" of the nation.

2) The federal government spent more than _____ on an ultra-modern radar network, called the _____. Soon Alaska's sparse communities became _____ in a way that never could have happened without _____ money.

3) They also brought _____ communications – as well as _____ marriages – that introduced new cultures to Native communities.

90

4) By the early 1950s, the tent city at the mouth of _____ had turned into a bustling, modern city thanks to _____.

5) The town which in 1947 didn't have one _____ light, found itself playing catch-up to a demand for _____. Reliable _____ for the growing populace soon became a major problem. _____ became frequent, prices were high and many homes had no _____ at all.

6) "An airline pilot, arriving over _____ at night after the long flight from Tokyo and seeing for the first time its pattern of flickering lights, winking like _____ in the midst of a vast, forbidding _____, described the city as a '_____.' In many respects, the name fits.

7) The National Municipal League and Look magazine named _____ an "_____" in 1956 for "successfully tackling a skyrocketing _____ that threatened to swamp city facilities and pushing for needed civic improvements." It was the first time that any city outside of the _____ had been so honored.

8) _____ persisted in the remote villages partly because _____ was sparse and partly because the conditions under which _____ lived was conducive to its spread. Segregation of active _____ cases was not easy among _____ because families were large and lived together in small spaces – often sleeping in the same bed.

9) Alaska _____ was used to set up control programs, establish a _____, administer _____ and deliver health services. Another _____ was used to build a _____ at Mount Edgecumbe near Sitka, a 400-bed hospital in Anchorage and 25-bed hospitals at _____ _____.

UNIT 6: COLD WAR ERA

UNIT TEST

Choose *two* of the following questions to answer in paragraph form. Use as much detail as possible to completely answer the question. Use extra paper in back of the book if needed.

1) How did the "red scare" put a spotlight on Alaska? How did it change Alaska?

2) Why did Anchorage's population increase dramatically in the 1950s? What problems did the city face because of the influx of people to the city?

3) Name two other Alaska towns that grew during the 1950s. How did these towns benefit by the defense spending during the 1950s?

4) Describe the tuberculosis crisis for Alaska Natives. Why was it so much worse for Alaska Natives than non-Natives? How did the government get involved in stopping the epidemic?

_____

_____

_____

_____

_____

_____

_____

_____

_____

_____

_____

_____

_____

_____

_____

_____

_____

_____

_____

UNIT 6: COLD WAR ERA

Review Questions   _____   (possible   6 pts.)
Fill-the-Blanks   _____   (possible   9 pts.)

Unit Test
Essay 1
Demonstrates understanding of the topic   _____   (possible 5 pts.)
Answered the questions completely and accurately   _____   (possible 5 pts.)
Composition is neat   _____   (possible 5 pts.)
Grammar and Spelling   _____   (possible 5 pts.)

Essay 2
Demonstrates understanding of the topic   _____   (possible 5 pts.)
Answered the questions completely and accurately   _____   (possible 5 pts.)
Composition is neat   _____   (possible 5 pts.)
Grammar and Spelling   _____   (possible 5 pts.)

Subtotal Points _____ (possible 55 pts.)

Extra Credit
Word Puzzle   _____   (5 pt. per completed puzzle)
Complete an Enrichment Activity   _____   (possible 5 pts.)
Oral presentation   _____   (possible 10 pts.)

Total Extra Credit   _____

Total Unit Points _____

GRADE CHART

A   50-55+ points

B   44-49 points

C   38-43 points

D   32-37 points

UNIT 7: ROAD TO STATEHOOD

LESSON 24: MOVERS & SHAKERS

FACTS TO KNOW

Judge James Wickersham – Introduced the first statehood bill for Alaska in 1916
Organic Act of 1884 – Allowed Alaska to become a civil and judicial territory
John Kinkead – Alaska's first governor, appointed by U.S. President Chester Arthur in 1884

COMPREHENSION QUESTIONS

1) What was the result of Alaska's first statehood bill in 1916? Why? _____
_____
_____
_____
_____

2) What event caused the government to pay more attention to Alaska in 1880?
_____
_____
_____
_____

3) What did the Organic Act of 1884 provide Alaska? _____
_____
_____
_____
_____

4) According to political scientist Melvin Crain, what were the responsibilities of the first governors of Alaska? _____
_____
_____
_____
_____

5) Describe the Civil Code of 1900 that Congress adopted after the Klondike gold rush.

_____
_____
_____
_____

6) What were some of Judge Wickersham's accomplishments that benefited Alaska?

_____
_____
_____
_____

DISCUSSION QUESTION

(Discuss this question with your teacher or write your answer in essay form below. Use additional paper if necessary.)

Why was statehood important to Alaskans?

_____
_____
_____
_____
_____
_____
_____
_____
_____
_____
_____
_____
_____
_____

ENRICHMENT ACTIVITY

Look for the book Frontier Politics: Alaska's James Wickersham by Evangeline Atwood at your local library. After you have read it, write a one-page report about what you learned.

LEARN MORE

Frontier Politics: Alaska's James Wickersham. Evangeline Atwood. Portland, Oregon: Binford & Mort, 1979.

UNIT 7: ROAD TO STATEHOOD

LESSON 25: STATEHOOD MOMENTUM BUILDS

FACTS TO KNOW

Territorial Gov. Ernest Gruening – Alaska's territorial governor from 1939-1953
Edward Lewis "Bob" Bartlett – Elected the territory's official delegate to Congress

COMPREHENSION QUESTIONS

1) Why did some oppose statehood for Alaska? _____
_____
_____
_____
_____

2) Why was Austin "Cap" Lathrop opposed to statehood? Why did his successor, C.W. Snedden, endorse statehood? _____
_____
_____
_____
_____

3) What events changed Gov. Ernest Gruening's opinion about statehood? _____
_____
_____
_____
_____

4) What did Gov. Gruening do to try to get statehood for Alaska? _____
_____
_____
_____
_____

5) Did President Harry S. Truman support statehood for Alaska? What did he tell Congress about the issue? _____

_____

_____

_____

6) How did the statehood bill get shut down by the Senate? _____

_____

_____

_____

DISCUSSION QUESTION

(Discuss this question with your teacher or write your answer in essay form below. Use additional paper if necessary.)

Many Alaskans fought hard to convince the government to grant statehood. Can you think of another time in history when people banded together to make an important change in the world?

_____

_____

_____

_____

_____

_____

_____

_____

_____

_____

_____

ENRICHMENT ACTIVITY

Imagine that you are a resident of Alaska living in the early 1900s. Write a persuasive letter to the U.S. president about why Alaska should have statehood. Include at least three detailed points to support your stance.

LEARN MORE

Alaska's Quest for Statehood 1867-1959. Robert A. Frederick. Anchorage: Anchorage Silver Anniversary Task Force, Municipality of Anchorage, 1985.

UNIT 7: ROAD TO STATEHOOD

LESSON 26: EGAN: THE FINAL PUSH

FACTS TO KNOW

William Allen Egan – Chairman of the Constitutional Convention and Alaska's first elected state governor; he was born in Valdez

Anthony J. Dimond – Alaska's non-voting delegate to Congress from 1932-1944

Constitutional Convention – Meeting of 55 volunteers from all walks of life in Fairbanks in 1955-1956 to draft a constitution for what they hoped would be a new state of Alaska

Frank Peratrovich – A Tlingit Indian from Southeast Alaska, and the only member of the Constitutional Convention that was Alaska Native, he was elected vice chairman of the Convention held in Fairbanks in 1955-1956

Alaska-Tennessee Plan – Provided Alaska with two senators and one representative to Congress; the same plan was used by Tennessee in 1796 to gain admission to the Union

COMPREHENSION QUESTIONS

1) How did William Egan get involved in politics? _____
_____
_____
_____
_____

2) Summarize Anthony Dimond's vision of Alaska as a state? _____
_____
_____
_____
_____

3) What qualifications did William Egan have to be elected president of the Constitutional Convention? _____
_____
_____
_____
_____

4) What were some of the terms of the state constitution that the delegates signed in 1956? _____

_____
_____
_____

5) Explain how the Alaska-Tennessee plan got its name? What was unique about the way that Alaska's prospective congressmen traveled to Washington D.C.? _____

_____
_____
_____

DISCUSSION QUESTION

(Discuss this question with your teacher or write your answer in essay form below. Use additional paper if necessary.)

How do you think Alaska would be different today if it never achieved statehood?

_____
_____
_____
_____
_____
_____
_____
_____
_____
_____
_____
_____
_____
_____
_____
_____

TIME TO REVIEW

Review Chapters 24-26 of your book before moving on the Unit Review. See how many questions you can answer without looking at your book.

UNIT 7: ROAD TO STATEHOOD

REVIEW LESSONS 24-26

Write down what you remember about:

Judge James Wickersham _____

_____

Organic Act of 1884 _____

_____

John Kinkead _____

_____

Territorial Gov. Ernest Gruening _____

_____

Edward Lewis "Bob" Bartlett _____

_____

William Allen Egan _____

_____

Anthony J. Dimond _____

_____

Constitutional Convention _____

_____

Frank Peratrovich _____

_____

Alaska-Tennessee Plan _____

_____

Fill in the blanks:

1) Through the _____, Congress provided Alaska with the bare essentials of government. It did not authorize a legislature, but it did make _____ the temporary capital and allowed for a _____.

2) Among Judge _____ accomplishments are winning home rule for Alaska as a _____ in 1912, obtaining funds for construction of the _____ in 1914, opening the _____ in 1917 – which later became the _____ – and introducing the first _____ bill in 1916, 43 years before it became a reality.

3) Proponents reasoned that statehood would allow Alaska to raise _____ and take over management of its _____. It also could establish a state-managed _____ force and state-appointed _____. In addition, Alaskans would get two _____ members in the U.S. Senate and one in the House of Representatives.

4) Those in opposition included powerful outside _____ companies that held monopolies in the territory and flowed profits to _____. There also were some influential Alaskans who didn't want to change the status quo – including _____, who owned the Fairbanks Daily News Miner.

5) _____, an Easterner appointed as Alaska's _____ from 1939-1953, became convinced that the only way Alaska would get adequate _____, and settle _____ rights, was to have elected, _____ representatives in Congress.

6) _____, the godson of Anthony J. Dimond, learned about American politics by faithfully reading the _____ during Dimond's stint in Washington, D.C. He also followed weekly Valdez Miner columns submitted by Dimond's secretary, _____, who became Alaska's delegate in 1944. Following in his godfather's Democratic Party footsteps, _____ won a seat in the Territorial House of Representatives in 1940.

7) _____ drafted the legislation calling for a 75-day _____ to be held on the campus of the University of Alaska in College, near Fairbanks, in November _____. He led the group in drafting Alaska's first _____.

8) Sen-elect _____ and Rep-elect Rivers traveled to Washington D.C. as part
of the _____ plan, which was used by _____
in 1796 to gain admission to the Union. It provided for the election of two _____
and one _____ to send to Congress.

**From left, Senator-elect Ernest Gruening, Martha Rivers, Representative-elect Ralph
Rivers, Neva Egan and Senator-elect William Egan stand by the car that the Rivers and
Egans drove all the way to the East Coast in order to present Congress with Alaska's newly
drafted 15-article constitution and Alaska-Tennessee Plan. They left Fairbanks on Dec. 10,
1956, and arrived in Washington, D.C., three weeks later. The group averaged 300 miles a
day with only snow tires, no chains, in 60-below-zero temperatures.**

Road to Statehood

Word Search Puzzle

Find the words listed below

```
E  H  D  R  F  S  M  U  A  T  P  Q  Q  J  Z  E  B  G  W  M
D  D  O  S  R  E  V  I  R  H  P  L  A  R  F  Y  Y  T  T  M
W  Q  O  I  D  C  P  A  H  B  O  Q  W  F  N  R  R  E  H  F
A  G  W  D  F  R  A  N  K  P  E  R  A  T  R  O  V  I  C  H
R  T  T  V  A  D  G  N  I  N  E  U  R  G  T  S  E  N  R  E
D  N  A  M  S  E  I  E  X  K  D  E  J  M  D  Z  E  M  Y  T
B  R  T  X  A  M  K  I  T  G  S  S  I  N  A  D  F  N  C  D
A  G  R  J  S  H  X  N  J  V  Y  K  O  F  N  T  Y  A  J  A
R  E  E  A  N  Y  S  U  I  V  B  M  O  V  D  L  W  L  N  U
T  X  B  M  V  S  P  R  H  K  I  Y  D  I  O  V  E  P  A  S
L  W  O  F  U  O  Q  L  E  D  N  L  C  N  Q  A  C  E  G  T
E  A  R  B  K  E  W  M  Y  K  R  H  O  D  D  V  P  E  E  I
T  N  U  H  A  W  L  N  P  U  C  R  O  L  D  H  S  S  M  N
T  G  W  I  K  S  O  Y  O  W  I  I  H  J  K  T  X  S  A  L
K  W  X  N  U  H  G  O  N  B  L  H  W  X  A  E  A  E  I  A
R  H  I  B  T  K  N  Z  O  G  H  L  P  S  R  J  G  N  L  T
S  C  L  N  P  P  R  X  I  M  W  W  Z  C  E  Q  Y  N  L  H
H  V  A  Z  V  Q  E  R  C  S  A  P  L  M  J  M  B  E  I  R
R  H  D  C  R  O  S  K  F  Q  I  B  Y  K  R  B  A  T  W  O
R  O  F  V  B  A  D  N  B  D  C  O  Z  T  N  M  K  J  L  P
```

WILLIAM EGAN	JAMES WICKERSHAM	ANTHONY DIMOND
JOHN KINKEAD	EDWARD BARTLETT	AUSTIN LATHROP
ERNEST GRUENING	ROBERT ATWOOD	FRANK PERATROVICH
RALPH RIVERS	TENNESSEE PLAN	

UNIT 7: ROAD TO STATEHOOD

UNIT TEST

Choose *two* of the following questions to answer in paragraph form. Use as much detail as possible to completely answer the question. Use extra paper in back of the book if needed.

1) Why was Judge James Wickersham considered one of the most influential Alaskans in history? Write about at least two of his accomplishments.

2) What were some of the arguments for and against statehood for Alaska? Share at least three of each.

3) How did William Egan make a difference in the fight for statehood before he was sworn into office?

_____

_____

_____

_____

_____

_____

_____

_____

_____

_____

_____

_____

_____

_____

_____

_____

_____

_____

_____

_____

_____

_____

UNIT 7: ROAD TO STATEHOOD

Review Questions   _____ (possible 10 pts.)
Fill-the-Blanks   _____ (possible 8 pts.)

Unit Test
Essay 1
Demonstrates understanding of the topic   _____ (possible 5 pts.)
Answered the questions completely and accurately   _____ (possible 5 pts.)
Composition is neat   _____ (possible 5 pts.)
Grammar and Spelling   _____ (possible 5 pts.)

Essay 2
Demonstrates understanding of the topic   _____ (possible 5 pts.)
Answered the questions completely and accurately   _____ (possible 5 pts.)
Composition is neat   _____ (possible 5 pts.)
Grammar and Spelling   _____ (possible 5 pts.)

Subtotal Points _____ **(possible 58 pts.)**

Extra Credit
Word Puzzle   _____ (5 pt. per completed puzzle)
Complete an Enrichment Activity   _____ (possible 5 pts.)
Oral presentation   _____ (possible 10 pts.)

Total Extra Credit   _____

Total Unit Points _____

GRADE CHART

A   53-58+ points

B   47-52 points

C   41-46 points

D   35-40 points

UNIT 8: STATEHOOD AT LAST

LESSON 27: BLACK GOLD TIPS THE BALANCE

FACTS TO KNOW

Kenai Peninsula – Where the discovery of oil began the petroleum boom

Thomas White – Known as the "Sourdough Driller" because he drilled the first producing oil well in Alaska

Katalla – City in the Kenai Peninsula that boomed after the first oil fields were discovered

COMPREHENSION QUESTIONS

1) Name two groups of people that discovered oil in Alaska before 1957. What did these groups use it for? _____

_____

_____

_____

2) How did Thomas White find the first producing oil field in Alaska? _____

_____

_____

_____

_____

3) How did the 1920 Mineral Leasing Act change the oil rush in Alaska? _____

_____

_____

_____

_____

4) What did Cook Inlet oil provide for Alaskans? _____

_____

_____

_____

_____

DISCUSSION QUESTION

(Discuss this question with your teacher or write your answer in essay form below. Use additional paper if necessary.)

What would your everyday life be like without oil?

_____
_____
_____
_____
_____
_____
_____
_____
_____
_____
_____
_____
_____
_____
_____
_____
_____

ENRICHMENT ACTIVITY

Watch this short YouTube video about oil discoveries in Alaska:
https://www.youtube.com/watch?v=LJgXgHh6las

LEARN MORE

Read more about the discovery of oil in Alaska by visiting
http://www.akhistorycourse.org/modern-alaska/oil-discovery-and-development-in-alaska

UNIT 8: STATEHOOD AT LAST

LESSON 28: WE'RE IN!

FACTS TO KNOW

Theodore F. "Ted" Stevens – Young attorney who served as a coordinator for Alaska and Hawaii statehood movements

U.S. President Dwight Eisenhower – Signed the official papers to make Alaska the 49th state in 1959

COMPREHENSION QUESTIONS

1) When did Alaska officially become a state? _____

_____

_____

_____

_____

2) How did the appointment of Fred Seaton as Secretary of the Interior in 1956 help the cause of statehood? _____

_____

_____

_____

_____

3) What did Theodore Stevens do to help Alaska receive statehood? _____

_____

_____

_____

_____

4) Name two other things that helped Alaska achieve statehood? _____

_____

_____

_____

_____

5) What were some of the tasks that William Egan had to handle after being elected as Alaska's first governor? _____

_____
_____
_____
_____

6) What happened to him shortly after he took the oath of office? _____

_____
_____
_____
_____

DISCUSSION QUESTION

(Discuss this question with your teacher or write your answer in essay form below. Use additional paper if necessary.)

Why did many people pity William Egan when he was elected as Alaska's first governor?

_____
_____
_____
_____
_____
_____
_____
_____
_____
_____
_____
_____

ENRICHMENT ACTIVITY

Using what you've learned from Units 6 and 7, create a timeline of events that led to Alaska gaining statehood in 1959.

LEARN MORE

A History of Alaska Statehood. Claus-M. Naske. Maryland: University Press of America, 1985.

UNIT 8: STATEHOOD AT LAST

LESSON 29: 'SIMPLE FLAG OF THE LAST FRONTIER'

FACTS TO KNOW

John Ben "Benny" Benson – Designed Alaska's flag in 1920
Willow ptarmigan – Official state bird of Alaska
Forget-me-not – Official state flower of Alaska
Alaska's Flag – Official song of Alaska written by Marie Drake

COMPREHENSION QUESTIONS

1) Where did Benny Benson grow up? What was he like as a young boy? _____

_____

_____

_____

_____

2) When did Benny Benson become fascinated with the stars? _____

_____

_____

_____

_____

3) How old was he when he designed the flag? Explain how his design was chosen.

_____

_____

_____

_____

4) How did he explain his design on his entry? _____

_____

_____

_____

5) How was Benny Benson honored at the signing of Alaska's constitution? _____

_____

_____

_____

DISCUSSION QUESTION

(Discuss this question with your teacher or write your answer in essay form below. Use additional paper if necessary.)

If you were asked to design the flag of Alaska, how would you draw it?

TIME TO REVIEW

Review Chapters 27-29 of your book before moving on the Unit Review. See how many questions you can answer without looking at your book.

Statehood At Last
Word Scramble Puzzle
Unscramble the words below

1. atdhtsoeo   What Alaska officially achieved on Jan. 3, 1959

2. hwitgd seinoreewh   U.S. President who signed the Alaska Statehood Bill

3. etd sensetv   Young attorney who became known as "Mr. Alaska"

4. lmailiw aeng   Alaska's first elected governor

5. daewdr eatrtltb   One of two first elected Alaska senators

6. rtsene rgnuneig   One of two first elected Alaska senators

7. rpahl sevrri   First elected Alaska congressman

8. huhg aewd   First Alaska lieutenant governor

9. otebrr owdoat   Editor of the Anchorage Daily Times

10. eatiiooarzgnnr llbi   This bill allowed the governor to appoint 12 commissioners for state departments

Statehood At Last
Word Scramble Puzzle
Unscramble the words below

#	Scramble	Clue
1.	vrroognes osnmani	Place where the Egan family lived in Juneau following statehood
2.	gaiiirnv nosma	Hospital in Seattle where Gov. Egan underwent surgery after taking office
3.	yebnn onnesb	Designer of the Alaska flag
4.	reiam eakdr	Author of the Alaska Flag song
5.	irnoel deusurbny	Creator of the melody for the Alaska Flag song
6.	olloap	Alaska's flag flew to the moon on board the 11th version of this spacecraft in July 1969 (when the first two humans actually walked on the moon)
7.	egoerg pkasr	Alaska territorial governor who initiated the flag contest for Alaska's school children
8.	ssjee ele	Home where Alaska's flag designer grew up
9.	fldoy niteugr	Alaska's first commissioner of administration
10.	dvzael	Town where Alaska's first elected governor was born

UNIT 8: STATEHOOD AT LAST

REVIEW LESSONS 27-29

Write down what you remember about:

Kenai Peninsula _____

_____

Thomas White _____

_____

Katalla _____

_____

Theodore F. "Ted" Stevens _____

_____

U.S. President Dwight Eisenhower _____

_____

John Ben "Benny" Benson _____

_____

Willow ptarmigan _____

_____

Forget-me-not _____

_____

Alaska's Flag _____

_____

Fill in the blanks:

1) In 1896, trapper _____ was bear hunting in the Controller Bay region near _____. He fell into thick, black mud seeping up from the ground. After cleaning his gun and himself, he _____ "to see what would happen," he later said. The pool _____ for a month. It became the first producing _____ discovered in Alaska.

2) _____ oil provided Alaskans with _____.
And a _____, built beneath Turnagain Arm, carried natural _____ from the Kenai Peninsula to heat Anchorage homes and businesses.

3) By 1957, _____ senators who had previously opposed admitting both Alaska and Hawaii as states because they feared new senators would not be sympathetic to _____, knew the tide had turned. Anti-_____ forces already had a clear majority.

4) And the discovery of a large _____ in the _____ Peninsula that December proved that Alaska probably would be able to carry its own _____ weight.

5) President _____ signed the official papers to make Alaska the _____ on Jan. 3, _____.

6) Alaskans love their _____, designed by half-Aleut _____
in the 1920s. Its simple design of _____ came from _____'s love of the _____ found in his homeland.

7) Perhaps his fascination with those distant twinkling stars inspired the _____-year-old _____ when his _____ teacher announced the territory-wide contest for school children to _____ for Alaska.

UNIT 8: STATEHOOD AT LAST

UNIT TEST

Choose *two* of the following questions to answer in paragraph form. Use as much detail as possible to completely answer the question. Use extra paper in back of the book if needed.

1) Who were the first groups of people to use oil in Alaska? What did they use it for? How did the "discovery" of oil in the Kenai Peninsula change Alaska?

2) Write a short summary of how Alaska officially became a state. What events led to the official signing of the documents by President Eisenhower in January 1959?

3) How was the design for Alaska's flag chosen? Who was the designer? How did he explain his design?

_____

_____

_____

_____

_____

_____

_____

_____

_____

_____

_____

_____

_____

_____

_____

_____

_____

_____

_____

_____

_____

UNIT 8: STATEHOOD AT LAST

Review Questions _____ (possible 9 pts.)
Fill-the-Blanks _____ (possible 7 pts.)

Unit Test
Essay 1
Demonstrates understanding of the topic _____ (possible 5 pts.)
Answered the questions completely and accurately _____ (possible 5 pts.)
Composition is neat _____ (possible 5 pts.)
Grammar and Spelling _____ (possible 5 pts.)

Essay 2
Demonstrates understanding of the topic _____ (possible 5 pts.)
Answered the questions completely and accurately _____ (possible 5 pts.)
Composition is neat _____ (possible 5 pts.)
Grammar and Spelling _____ (possible 5 pts.)

Subtotal Points _____ **(possible 56 pts.)**

Extra Credit
Word Puzzle _____ (5 pt. per completed puzzle)
Complete an Enrichment Activity _____ (possible 5 pts.)
Oral presentation _____ (possible 10 pts.)

Total Extra Credit _____

Total Unit Points _____

GRADE CHART

A   51-56+ points

B   45-50 points

C   39-44 points

D   33-38 points

EXTRA PAPER FOR LESSONS

EXTRA PAPER FOR LESSONS

EXTRA PAPER FOR LESSONS

EXTRA PAPER FOR LESSONS

EXTRA PAPER FOR LESSONS

EXTRA PAPER FOR LESSONS

EXTRA PAPER FOR LESSONS

EXTRA PAPER FOR LESSONS

EXTRA PAPER FOR LESSONS

EXTRA PAPER FOR LESSONS

EXTRA PAPER FOR LESSONS

Made in the USA
Monee, IL
19 September 2021